THE ALMOST TRUE ADVENTURES OF TYTUS THE MONKEY

WRITTEN & ILLUSTRATED BY
TOBY PRICE

The Almost True Adventures of Tytus the Monkey

Copyright © by Toby Price
Second edition 2023

All rights reserved.

No part of this publication may be reproduced in any form, or by any means, electronic or mechanical, including photocopying, recording, or any information browsing, storage or retrieval system, without permission in writing from the publisher.

www.codebreakeredu.com

This book is dedicated to my lovely wife, Leah.

Twenty-two years ago during my first visit to your apartment, I found my "Say Anything" VHS tape on your shelf. I knew right then I would do whatever it took to win your heart, and get my movie back. Thank you for making me a husband, a dad, and a much better person than I ever dreamed I could become.

I love you more than books.

People always said Tytus the Monkey was evil.
It was because he was always causing trouble.

He couldn't stand it when people were singing.

He felt like most other animals thought they were better than him.

But Tytus didn't dislike everything.
In fact, he loved the children that adopted him as their own.
They taught him so many things.

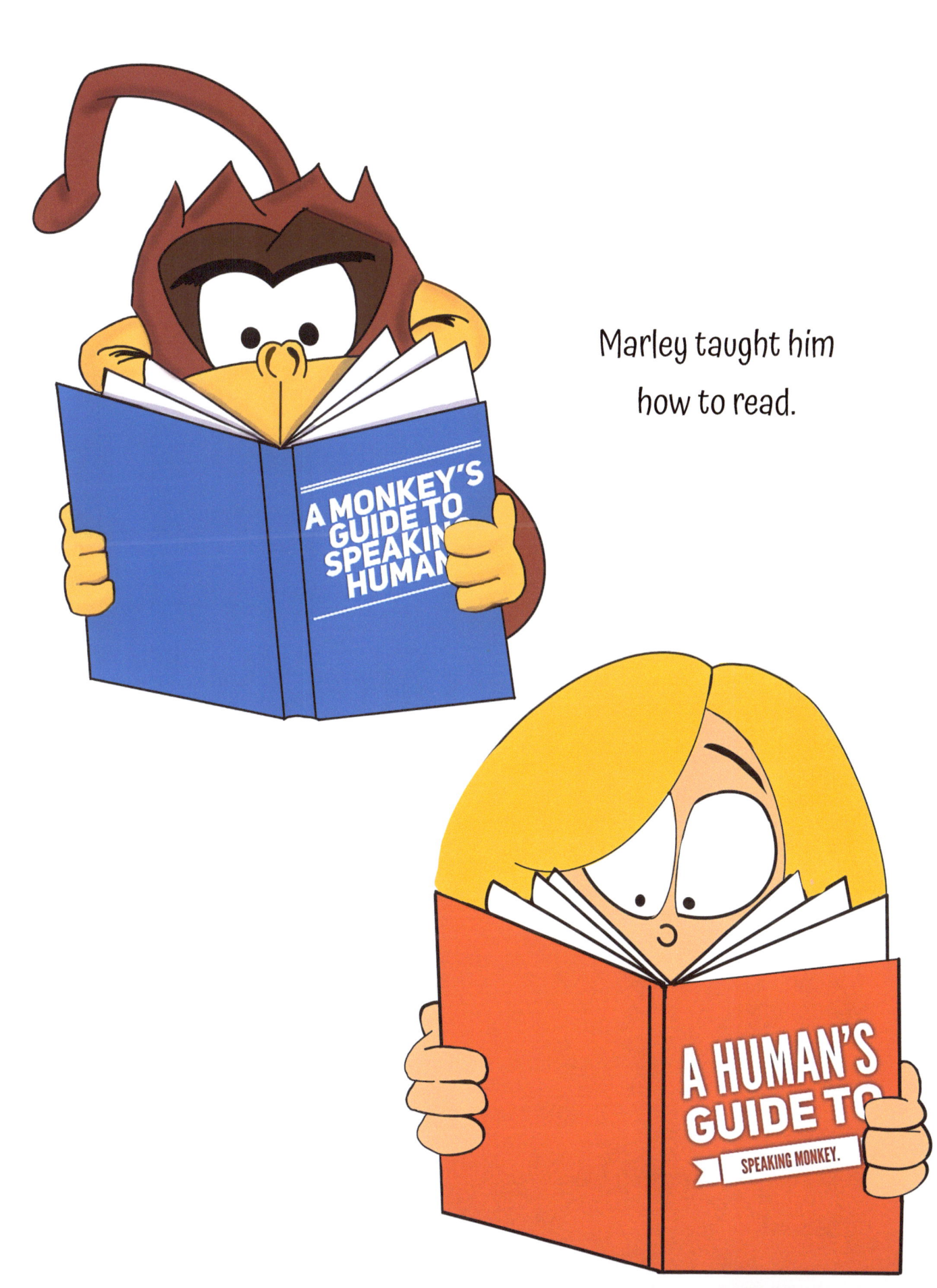

Marley taught him how to read.

Addison taught him about art.

McKade taught him how to roller skate.

Tytus and his kids had many things in common.

They loved climbing to high places.

They loved swimming.

They loved drinking slushies.

They loved eating pancakes.

Most of all, they loved going to the store.

Tytus and McKade loved the way the doors would open with a big

WOOSH!

Everyone would find their spot around the shopping cart.
Today, everything was going great...

**until...
it wasn't.**

The lights in the store were too **BUZZY!**

The registers at the front were too

BEEPY!

Tytus jumped in front of Addison. He knew what was happening. Her hands started flapping. Her eyes began to blink. And then she started to cry. She sounded just like a siren. All of the lights and sounds were making her so uncomfortable.

"She has autism," the kids' mom told her. "She gets overwhelmed and can't always tell us why because she doesn't talk very well."

HRMPH!

The lady who smelled like cheese was not very nice and replied, "Just because she can't talk, doesn't mean you can't teach her some manners."

Tytus did not always understand why people said what they said, but he knew that the lady who smelled like cheese was not nice. That bothered Tytus more than bugs, singing, and snooty animals.

The lady who smelled like cheese gave Tytus an **IDEA!**

I can't talk but I can definitely teach that lady a lesson!

he thought to himself.

Tytus crept over to the lady's shopping cart. He took the top off of her dish soap and turned it upside down.

The soap started to

DRIP!

DROP!

PLOP!

onto the floor.

When the lady who smelled like cheese put one foot into the soapy puddle, she fell into her shopping cart and slid all the way across the floor.

She crashed into the cage-free eggs.
The eggs tumbled onto a store employee carrying
a crate of apples.

The store employee dropped the apples and the crate went

CRACK

as it exploded on the floor.

The kids' mom stumbled on the apples and lost control of her shopping cart!

McKade **ZOOMED** down the aisle toward the milk display.

The cart crashed into the milk with a loud

BOOM!

The tall milk tower started to lean.

It **teetered.** It **tottered.**

It **toppled** over on the stacks of soda.

The crazy collision caused a gigantic tidal wave that covered everyone! The entire back of the store was a slippery, slimy, soupy mess.

Tytus thought this was hilarious...

until...

it wasn't.

...uh oh...

Just before everyone's tempers detonated, Addison walked over to the lady who smelled like cheese (and now eggs). She offered the lady a paper towel and helped her back to her feet.

McKade started to put the lady's groceries back into her cart. Marley grabbed some paper towels and started to hand them out to everyone.

Slowly, all of the people in the store started to talk, clean up, and laugh about what just happened.

Addison may not be able to speak, but she taught Tytus a lesson that day. If you are out in the world and can't find a nice person, you should be one.

Epilogue...

WHAT IS SENSORY OVERLOAD?

In the story, Addison becomes very upset in the grocery store. She is overwhelmed by things in her environment. The loud registers, buzzy lights, and bangy carts cause her to go into sensory overload. Sensory Overload is when your senses—sound, sight, taste, touch, smell—take in more information than your brain can process. When overwhelmed by all of the input, the brain reacts like it would to a life threatening situation. It can cause a person to fight, freeze, or run away.

There are many things that can cause someone to feel overwhelmed by their environment. Some examples are:

- Cooking smells
- Fire alarms
- Sirens (Fire Trucks, Police Cars, Ambulances)
- Hand dryers
- Different soaps
- New clothes
- Vacuum cleaners
- Large groups of people

Some examples of things you can do to help someone that is feeling overwhelmed by their environment are:

- Noise reducing headphones
- Weighted blankets
- Dimming the lights in a room
- Taking a break alone
- Scents that the person enjoys

The most important thing to remember is to always be patient and kind.

ABOUT THE AUTHOR

Toby Price is a lifelong educator and school leader. He is a proud husband, dad, story teller, artist, and King of Dad Jokes. He believes all kids need to see themselves in books and stories. He also advocates to ensure kids have access to all kinds of books, especially silly books. You can find him online discussing everything from autism, education, Spiderman, Star Wars, fart jokes, and jigsaw puzzles. Toby lives with his wife of twenty-two years and three kids in Mississippi.

Toby insists that Tytus the Monkey is not real. He did not sneak away from a petting zoo, then ride in Price's moving truck from Ohio to Mississippi. If you run into Tytus in public do not give him cookies or soda, no matter what he tells you.

CODE BREAKER LEADERSHIP SERIES

 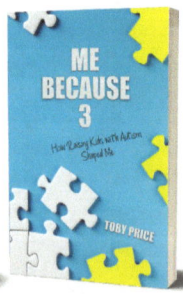    

CODE BREAKER KID COLLECTION

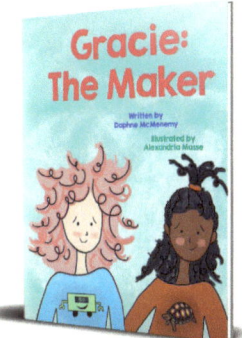
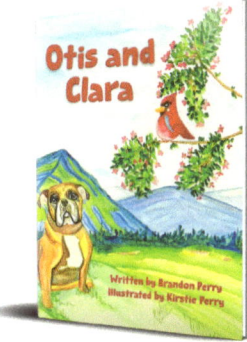

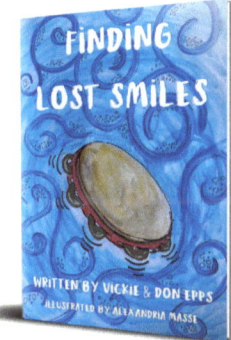

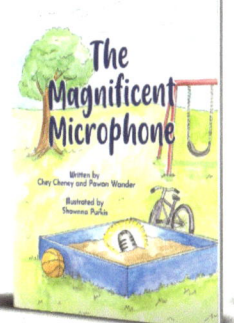
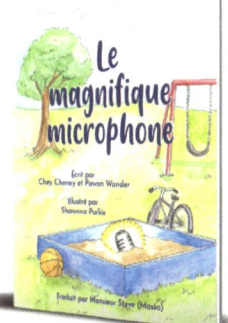
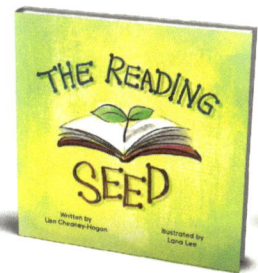